ANIMALS AT RISK
WHALES IN DANGER

BY MICHAEL PORTMAN

Gareth Stevens
Publishing

Please visit our website, www.garethstevens.com. For a free color catalog of all our high-quality books, call toll free 1-800-542-2595 or fax 1-877-542-2596.

Library of Congress Cataloging-in-Publication Data

Portman, Michael, 1976-
Whales in danger / Michael Portman.
      p. cm. — (Animals at risk)
Includes index.
ISBN 978-1-4339-5816-8 (pbk.)
ISBN 978-1-4339-5817-5 (6-pack)
ISBN 978-1-4339-5814-4 (library binding)
1. Whales—Juvenile literature. 2. Endangered species—Juvenile literature. I. Title.
QL737.C4P667 2012
599.5—dc22

                                   2011013326

First Edition

Published in 2012 by
Gareth Stevens Publishing
111 East 14th Street, Suite 349
New York, NY 10003

Copyright © 2012 Gareth Stevens Publishing

Designer: Haley W. Harasymiw
Editor: Therese M. Shea

Photo credits: Cover, pp. 1, 4, 5, 11, 13, 15 Shutterstock.com; p. 7 Thomas Haider/Oxford Scientific/Getty Images; p. 9 David B. Fleetham/Oxford Scientific/Getty Images; p. 17 Brandon Hauser/Science Faction/Getty Images; p. 19 David McNew/Getty Images.

Printed in the United States of America

CPSIA compliance information: Batch #CS11GS: For further information contact Gareth Stevens, New York, New York at 1-800-542-2595.

CONTENTS

Words in the glossary appear in **bold** type the first time they are used in the text.

GREAT WHALES OF THE OCEAN

Whales spend their whole lives in the water, but they aren't fish—they're **mammals**. Unlike fish, whales must swim to the surface to breathe air.

Whales belong to a group of animals called cetaceans. This group also includes dolphins and **porpoises**. There are at least 75 **species** of cetaceans.

Whale species are divided into two groups: toothed whales and baleen whales. Seven whale species are currently **endangered**. They may become **extinct** unless people take action.

killer whale

All cetaceans, such as these dolphins, have sleek bodies that easily glide through water.

WILD FACTS

Most people don't think of dolphins and porpoises as whales. However, scientists do because dolphins and porpoises have the same body features as whales.

TOOTHED WHALES

As their name suggests, toothed whales have teeth. Killer whales, or orcas, are toothed whales. So are dolphins and porpoises. Toothed whales eat fish, squid, octopus, and other sea animals.

The sperm whale is the largest toothed whale. It can grow to be 60 feet (18 m) long. However, most toothed whales are smaller than baleen whales.

Toothed whales have an opening on top of their head called a blowhole. A blowhole works like a **nostril**. It opens to allow air into and out of the whale's lungs.

Whales, such as the sperm whale below, can't breathe through their mouth. They use blowholes to breathe.

WILD FACTS

Baleen whales have two blowholes.

BALEEN WHALES

Baleen whales get their name from comb-like plates called baleen in their mouth. These plates are made of the same matter our fingernails are. Most baleen whales feed by taking big gulps of water and using the baleen to remove sea creatures, such as **krill** and small fish, from the water.

Blue whales are a kind of baleen whale. They're the largest whales. They can grow to over 100 feet (30 m) long and weigh as much as 200 tons (181 t). Blue whales can eat 4 to 8 tons (3.6 to 7.3 t) of krill a day!

Blue whales are the largest animals that have ever lived.

WILD FACTS

A blue whale's tongue is so big that an elephant could stand on it.

SOUND SWIMMERS

Whales have good eyesight and excellent hearing. Toothed whales make sounds that bounce off underwater objects. The whales use the **echoes** to find food and to avoid danger. This is called **echolocation**. Echolocation is especially useful in dark and cloudy water where whales can't see well.

Humpback whales—which are baleen whales—make sounds called whale songs. They probably sing to let other whales know they're near. However, scientists don't think baleen whales use echolocation.

WILD FACTS
Gray whales travel over 12,000 miles (19,300 km) as they swim from Alaska to Mexico and back each year.

Whales, such as these killer whales, live in groups called pods.

WHALE HUNTING

Humans have hunted whales for hundreds of years. Whale fat, called blubber, was used to make soap and oil for lamps and candles. Baleen was used to make products such as tennis rackets, umbrellas, and hats. Today, whale hunting, or whaling, is mostly for the animals' meat.

In 1986, the group responsible for watching over whalers banned whaling to allow whale populations to grow again. However, countries such as Japan, Iceland, and Norway have found ways around the ban and continue to hunt whales.

WILD FACTS

Each year, whalers kill more than 1,000 whales.

It's thought that whales can live to be 100 years old if they escape the dangers of the ocean.

POLLUTION

Whales are also at risk from many types of pollution. Dangerous **chemicals** and metals make their way into the oceans. Some are dumped into the water. Some leak into the ground and then spread from the ground into the ocean. Small amounts of toxic chemicals can end up in the sea creatures that are eaten by whales. Since whales eat such large amounts of food, dangerous amounts of those chemicals can build up in their bodies. The metal mercury, for example, does great harm to the brains of mammals and hurts their chances of having babies.

Whales are found in every ocean of the world. These humpback whales travel great distances each year.

Thousands of ships carrying people and goods travel the world's oceans and rivers. Unfortunately, these ships sometimes hit whales. Fast-moving boats can seriously hurt or even kill whales. In addition, the noise made by boat traffic is loud and can confuse them.

Fishing nets can catch whales by mistake. When a whale gets twisted in a fishing net and can't come to the surface for air, it drowns. Nets can also get wrapped around a whale's mouth so it can't eat.

WILD FACTS

Ships are the cause of an *estimated* 90 percent of the deaths of young Northern right whales.

Since many whales depend on echolocation to find food, noise from boats can scare them away from feeding areas.

17

OIL SPILLS AND DRILLING

If a whale surfaces in water covered with oil, it can suck the toxic oil into its lungs. Oil can plug its blowhole, making it hard or impossible for the whale to breathe. Oil spills can also poison or kill the whales' food supply.

Oil drilling can be dangerous to whales as well. Underwater explosions are used in building oil wells. These noises can severely harm a whale's hearing. Since whales depend so much on their hearing, this can change their lives and put them in danger.

Some whales travel the same path each year for food or to have babies. If oil wells are in this path, the journey becomes harder.

SAVING THE WHALES

Fortunately, many groups are working with governments around the world to stop pollution, improve oil-drilling safety, and end whaling. They hope these efforts, along with many others, will save whales.

The loss of even a small number of whales can have a big effect on whale populations. Female whales give birth to only a few babies in their lifetime. This means that it can take a long time for a whale population to grow. Gray whales were once near extinction, but **conservation** efforts saved them. Hopefully, the same can be done for all whales.

Seven Endangered Whale Populations

Species	Location	Estimated Number
right whale	eastern North Pacific Ocean	30
right whale	eastern North Atlantic Ocean	30
sei whale	Pacific Ocean	130
gray whale	western North Pacific Ocean	100
bowhead whale	North Atlantic Ocean	450
blue whale	North Atlantic Ocean	500
fin whale	western North Atlantic Ocean	1,600

GLOSSARY

chemical: matter that can be mixed with other matter to cause changes

conservation: the care of the natural world

echo: a sound that repeats because it bounces off an object

echolocation: a way of locating objects with echoes

endangered: in danger of dying out

estimated: describing a guess based on knowledge or facts

extinct: having no living members

krill: a tiny ocean creature that looks like a shrimp

mammal: an animal that has live young and feeds them milk from the mother's body

nostril: one of two openings at the end of the nose

porpoise: a toothed sea mammal that has a rounded nose and a triangular fin

species: a group of animals that are all of the same kind

FOR MORE INFORMATION

BOOKS

Hoare, Philip. *The Whale: In Search of the Giants of the Sea.* New York, NY: Ecco, 2010.

Kelsey, Elin. *Watching Giants: The Secret Lives of Whales.* Berkeley, CA: University of California Press, 2009.

Spilsbury, Louise, and Richard Spilsbury. *Blue Whale.* Chicago, IL: Heinemann Library, 2006.

WEBSITES

Blue Whales
kids.nationalgeographic.com/kids/animals/creaturefeature/blue-whales/
Watch videos and see pictures of blue whales.

Mammals: Whale
www.sandiegozoo.org/animalbytes/t-whale.html
Read facts about the lives of whales.

Whales and Dolphins
www.worldwildlife.org/species/finder/cetaceans/whalesanddolphins.html
Learn what's being done to save whales.

INDEX